Backyard Chickens:

Beginner's Guide to Feeding, Caring and

Raising Chickens for Eggs

Table of content:

Introduction: Don't be a Chicken! Here Are a Few Tips to Get Started!

Doing anything for the first time can present itself as a daunting task, but the good thing about raising backyard chickens is you don't have to do everything all at once. Everything you do will come in certain preordained steps, typically you have to have one stage of the process done before you advance on to the next. Allow me to lay out all of them for you right now. Because you don't have to be a chicken, you just need a few tips to get you started!

Handling Potential Permits and Fees

Depending on where you live you may have to pay a fee in order to get your permit to raise chickens. In some locales, the permit fee is as little as five dollars. If you have the bare minimum of pocket change, in most places you can get yourself an official permit to raise chickens. Along with this permit often comes a signed agreement to allow your property to be subjected to annual inspections.

This is not a big deal; it usually simply entails one local animal control officer swinging by the premise to take a look at your chicken coop. After a few minutes of a cursory inspection, the officer will give you the all clear and be on his way. The sooner you understand how to handle potential permits and fees; the sooner you can get started on raising your chickens.

Urban areas mostly require backyard chicken farmers to have no more than 3 or 4 chickens. But if you live in an agricultural area, you will be allowed to have twice that many. Once you know how many chickens you can have, you can start preparing your coop accordingly. You won't know how big to build it after all, until you know just how many chickens will be inside the coop to begin with. Check with your city board or council to find out just how many chickens you can legally have.

Be Aware of Distance Regulations

Distance relations can be a bit of a nuisance at times, but these are laws that were created with the welfare of your chickens—as well as your most immediate neighbors—welfare in mind.

Some towns however, do not have the clearest of restrictions in place, so you really have to check with the local powers that be to figure out how far away you need to keep your chickens. The local administrators can pull up official ordinance that state exactly how far away your chicken coop needs to be from neighboring property lines and local businesses. You may find that your area does not have any such restrictions at all, but you have to ask first.

Figure Out Zoning Rules

Before you get your chickens, you should educate yourself on the zoning rules of your community. If your property is zoned to be an "agricultural" region, you shouldn't have any trouble having chickens at all. But for those who are zoned as "residential, business, or urban" you will have to consider the applicable zoning rules that apply. The sooner you do so, the sooner you can get that chicken coop up and running.

Tell Your Neighbors

There are still three mainstay methods of communication among humans; there is "television", "telephone", and "tele-neighbor". And if you have ever had a nosy neighbor, you know full well that it is the latter of which that seems to cause the most widespread influence!

The best way to handle your neighbors is to employ as much open honesty as possible. Include these neighbors in on your building plans so they know what to expect. If you have a neighbor that is hard to deal with you can even hire a professional intermediary such as lawyer to discuss the finer details.

Chapter 1: The Benefits of Backyard Chicken Farming

There are plenty of benefits that can be derived from backyard chicken farming. So many in fact, you probably couldn't list them all in one book! In this chapter however, we are going to sum up the most important for you. I hope that the many benefits presented here will serve as encouragement and reinforcement as you get started on your backyard chicken farming adventure!

Chickens are Cheap

If you are on a tight budget, then chicken farms may be appealing simply because they are fairly cheap to get and even cheaper to maintain. You won't break the bank buying your chickens.

Eggs, Eggs, and More Eggs!

In case you didn't realize it, eggs come from chickens. And these chickens if taken care of well, will produce a lot of them. The eggs they produce are full of protein, and free from growth hormones. These natural eggs are not tampered with and come to as is, so that you can enjoy nature's supply of eggs without all of the added benefits that only home grown from the coop can provide.

Chickens Provide Healthy Meat

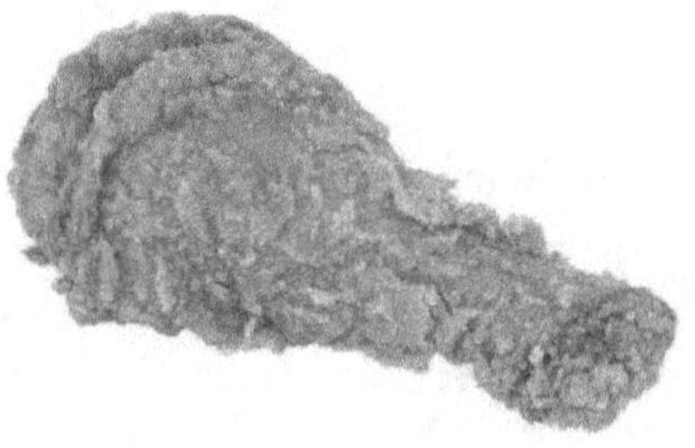

It goes without saying that chickens provide quality meat. More people eat meat from chicken than any other meat source on the planet. Chicken is healthier than red meat, and since your free-range chickens are grown naturally without any artificial chemicals added, they very well could be the healthiest meat of your entire diet.

Chickens Can Make Money

There are several ways that chickens can make you a lot of money. Chickens lay eggs which can be sold at competitive rate, and they also produce meat, which is very much in demand. Another way to make money off your chickens is to enter them into chicken show contests where you can often win cash prizes. There is more than one way for a chicken to make you some money.

These Backyard Birds Are Smart!

Did you know that chickens are incredibly smart? Chickens are one of the animal world's best communicators, they have 24 main sounds, and they are literally born with the gift of gab.

As soon as these birds hatch they begin to communicate specific information. Incredibly, even before they hatch, research has shown, that there is specific call the birds make to their mother. One repetitive bird calls these unhatched chickens make is to tell their bird mom to turn their egg over because their getting too cold!

It has been observed that these birds will squawk from within the eggs and like clockwork the bird's mother will dutifully turn the egg over! Anyone who has raised chickens also knows the distinctive cries for help that their chickens make. If the birds are at all disturbed by a potential predator, they will let you know with a specific series of bird calls that they only make in that threatening situation. These birdies not only have a good vocabulary however; they also have quite an ability when it comes to numbers.

Believe it or not, chickens just might be the only animal on this planet that can count! It has long been one of the wonders of the animal world, but yes, these birds know their arithmetic! It has been shown in many experiments that when chicken feed is placed in a specifically numbered spot, the birds will routinely return to that numbered spot, counting out the spaces to know exactly which spot has the feed.

And it isn't just counting numbers that these birds are capable, but apparently full-blown geometry! Because the same exact experiment has been replicated with geometric shapes! If the experimenters put out 12 bowls of chicken feed, each with a different geometric shape, the birds will remember the shapes to get to the food. Time and time again they could keep all 11 of the 12-bowls empty, but have a bowl with a triangle full, and the birds would make a beeline to the triangle bowl! These backyard birds are smart!

They Provide Fertilizer

Chickens are one of the greatest manure producers in the world. Chicken manure as fertilizer, when sprinkled evenly over a garden will help the veggies to sprout up in no time. To be blunt, these birds poop a lot and regularly manufacture about 85 pounds of manure pure bird, every single year. Of course, all this chicken poop is not something that is going to be appreciated unless you grow vegetables and use it as fertilizer. If you do however, you will be amazed at the results., and quickly realize just how much this bird crap is worth!

Chicken poop as organic fertilizer immediately bonds with the soil replenishing and nourishing it with a highly concentrated amount of nitrogen, to facilitate maximum growth. If you are having trouble getting your tomatoes to grow, just have your chickens poop on it and they will be sprouting up in no time! It may not always look pretty, but the truth is, these birds provide awesome fertilizer!

Chapter 2: Picking Your Chicken

I can remember when I was a kid and would visit a local farm to see freshly hatched chicks, the most important thing in picking one out would have been which one was the cutest! But as you grow into the role of a professional chicken farmer you begin to take notice of some more important key features of the birds. Depending on what it is you plan to use the birds for it is important to know which ones are good for eggs, which ones are good for meat, which ones are good for show, and so on and so forth. In this chapter we will explore all of the criteria involved when it comes to picking your chicken.

Chickens for Eggs

Having chickens that can regularly produce plenty of eggs is of great benefit and a highly sought-after attribute for most chicken farmers. And if this is going to be your primary purpose for having chickens there are a few types of birds in particular that can help you maximize your results. It is usually breeds that are known as "hybrid hens" that lay the most eggs. Among these, the most widely used hybrid is one humorously called the, "Golden Comet".

These breeds can produce a large volume of eggs without having to consume too much chicken feed in the process. These birds can typically produce about 280 eggs every single year. As their name might imply, the "Golden Comet" is usually yellow, or gold in color, with fluffy feathers. If you need a chicken to make you some eggs, be on the lookout for this birdie.

Chickens for Meat

If you are not worried about egg production and instead want to focus on the meatiest of chickens, there are a few options available for you. Most of the chicken consumed in North America come from what are known as "fast growing" chickens. These birds grow large at an incredible rate, usually reaching maximum size and weight at just 4 to 6 weeks. The fact that these animals have such a short life before being harvested of their meat is of course a bone of contention among many animal rights activists.

But truth be told, this is the best kind of bird to breed for meat. Among these rapid growers it is the "Cornish Cross" that seems to yield the best, most consistent results. In about 6 weeks these birds can weigh in at as much as 12 pounds. This is more than enough meat to go to market. And according to most, the Cornish Cross seems to have the best taste, making it the standard bearer for chicken meat.

Chickens for both Eggs and Meat

Now if you want a good multitasking chicken who can capably produce suitable eggs and meat, you will want to pick a bird that is known as a "dual purpose" chicken. One of the best dual-purpose birds you could ever use is one called the "Rhode Island Red". This bird can lay as much as 250 eggs a year and full-grown weighs in anywhere between 5 to 7 pounds. That makes this bird great for both eggs and meat as well. If you need this kind of duality in your chickens, you will need a bird such as this in order to succeed.

Chickens for Show

If you are concerned neither with egg or meat production but want to primarily focus on a show bird instead. You will want a bird that grows eye catching feathers and with a bit of spunk. A bird that perfectly fits that bill is the "Cubalaya". If you didn't guess it from the name, this bird hails from Cuba, and is known for its flashy blue, red, and black color scheme. Unlike some of their short lived meaty brethren, these birds do take a long time to mature, sometimes as much as 3 years. So, if you are in it for the long haul to get a bird to show off at the fair, get a bird like the Cubalaya and you will have quite a chicken to show!

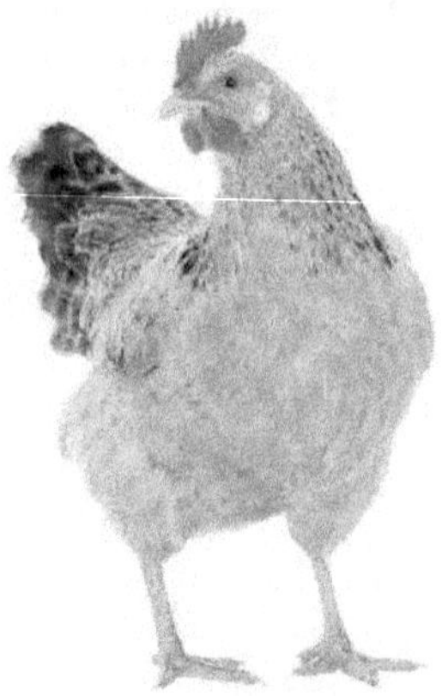

Instead of painting your eggs this Easter, how about having a chicken lay them for you already blazing with color? For some chicken eggs with a bit of flair, you will have to pick out your chickens accordingly. By far, the most reliable breed for this task is the aptly named, "Easter Egger", this renowned birdie can regularly lay eggs that are blue, green, and even pink! Talk to your local breeder to find out more!

Chapter 3: Buying Vs. Building a Coop

It is a fact of backyard chicken life, if you are going to have some chickens, then you are going to need a coop! The real question is however—should you buy a coop, or should you build your own? In this chapter we will focus on the pros and cons of both!

Reasons to Buy a Coop

Usually the biggest hurdle when it comes to buying a chicken coop is the cost. But if you can afford shelling out at least 300 dollars then you may be better off buying. Buying a coop comes ready made after all, and allows you to get to work with our chickens right away. Building coops is not for everyone, and if you are not technically inclined, you may not feel comfortable building one yourself. If this is the case for you, and all of these attributes sound familiar, then you should probably should consider buying a coop, rather than building one.

Reasons to Build a Coop

If you like to work with your hands, and you would much rather save your pocket money for something a bit more enjoyable. Then feel free to take it to the next level and build yourself a coop. Another reason to build your own, is that you can get creative in ways that a pre-built coop simply would not allow. Whatever you buy after all, you are basically stuck with. If you build your coop from the ground up however, you can create it however you like. Do you want your coop to have two chicken runs, 8-foot fencing, and a moat for good measure? Well—knock yourself out! Because if you build it, you can do it!

Good Places to Buy

If you would prefer to buy your own chicken coop there are plenty of places you can purchase them from. Even Wal-Mart is known to sell a batch of pre-made coops. Some of the best places to buy them are at garden supply stores, pet shops, and online. Order them direct from Amazon and you can have them shipped right to your door.

<u>*Coop Building in Brief*</u>

Start off by building a rectangular foundation, laying concrete down on the ground. Insert four 4 x 4 boards of wood into the concrete. Cut the front boards down to feet in height, and make the back boards 6 feet in height. This will give your roof a nice slant. Now just lay some additional 4 x 4's down for the roof, craft a little door and a chicken run, and your birds will rule the roost!

Chapter 4: What You Need for Chicken Feed

As living, breathing creatures, it goes without saying that your chickens will need to eat. But you can't just feed these little guys anything, you need to know precisely what, when and how these birds should eat. In this chapter we will go over some of the finer details when it comes to what you need for chicken feed.

How Much Do Chickens need to Eat?

To put it very simply, some chickens eat more than others. And in addition to this, in order for egg laying chickens to produce quality eggs they most have abundant nutrition. So, it is very important to make sure they are all routinely fed. This is why for egg laying birds, it is typically recommended that you give them the run of their own feeder. That means you should just leave a self-feeder out and let the birds eat as much as they want. Don't worry, these chickens aren't pigs, they know when their full and will only eat what they need.

Learn to Ration Out Chicken Feed

If you decide that you do need to ration out your chicken feed however, you should do it methodically and with a purposeful plan. If you are raising a bird for meat, you will have to keep in mind that it takes about 2 pounds of chicken feed in order to create 1 pound of meat on the bodies of your chickens. In standard rationing you should feed the birds in the morning and later in the night.

Also helpful for the chickens would be to add a little bit of grit to the feed dish every now and then. When we say "grit" we mean small little rock pebbles that the birds like to swallow with their food. Yes—if you see your birds eating rocks don't be alarmed! It's something they do naturally, and the rocky grit actually helps them to digest food.

Meal Time for Free Ranging Birds

If you are feeding free range birds, the regimen couldn't be easier. You are basically just trying to get your birds to begin eating just as they would in the wild. Just liberally sprinkle your feed in your backyard and let these birdies get to work.

Distributing Water with Your Feed

Chickens—like all living creatures—need to have plenty of water. But there are a few things you need to know when it comes to distributing water with your chicken's feed. Number one, you should always have water at the ready for your birds. This usually means having a water dropper so that they can suck out the water whenever they need it. Water droppers also prevent bullying among the birds.

You see, when left with other water distribution methods, such as a big bowl for them to drink out of, the birds tend to crowd around and shove each other, and the bigger birds just might completely block the smaller of the bunch. So, to make a long story short, in order to prevent the creation of some barnyard bird bullies, you might want to invest in a water dropper.

Chapter 5: Chicken Health and Maintenance

Healthy chickens mean healthy eggs, and healthy meat, it's a simple matter of calculus and simply can't be beat! In this chapter we will run through all of the most important aspects of chicken health and maintenance.

A Brief Word on Bird Flu

Bird Flu is a very serious viral infection that can infest just about any kind of bird it comes in contact with, whether wild or on the farm. The birds are often infected when they are moved from place to place, such as fairgrounds and the like, encountering other groups of chickens who then spread the disease on to them. But more commonly they get acquainted with the disease through what you track in with your shoes.

Potent strains of bird flu can live in bird feces for several days. This means that if some random bird with the virus craps on the sidewalk and you step in it, you could easily spread the germs to your coop just by stepping inside. Having that said, the best way to prevent an outbreak of bird flu just might be to wipe your feet!

How to Know if Your Chicken is Sick

The first step in knowing if one of your birds is sick is to have a proactive policy of inspecting them in the first place. You should make it a habit of checking out your birds once a week just to make sure they are doing alright. This entails a thorough examination of their feathers, legs, claws, eyes and head. Searching through the feathers you are looking for any parasites such as small black bugs that might be hiding there. Always be sure to use gloves when searching through your bird's feathers so that you can avoid contact with anything you might find.

Besides examining the bird's body for parasites, you should also be on the look out for any strange behavior, the bird is scratching itself constantly for example, this is a clear indication of mites, fleas, or lice. If the bird is being very still and sitting in the corner for long periods of time, on the other hand, your bird is probably sick with a cold, flue, or something potentially even more harmful. If you see any of these signs, you might want to consider the possibility that your chickens are sick.

Quarantining Birds and Managing Contagion

Since many illnesses can spread rather rapidly, it is of the utmost importance to quarantine a sick bird as soon as possible. This means taking the bird out of the coop entirely, and placing it in a walled off, separate holding area. This can be achieved with a simple cage from the pet store, or you could build your own makeshift holding area in an isolated spot on the yard.

Prevent Parasitic infection

The best way to prevent your chickens from being infected with parasites is to keep them and their living space as clean as possible. As dreadful as it may be, this means that you have to commit yourself to cleaning their chicken coop on a regular basis. No one likes spending their weekends knee deep in chicken poop, but if it means you will be able to keep your birds healthy it's worth it.

Chapter: 6: Securing and Protecting Your Chickens from Predators

I don't mean to scare you, but there are many plenty of threats lurking right in your backyard ready to snatch your chickens right from the coop. What are these sneaking predators skulking in the background of your chicken houses? Here in this chapter we will go down the list! Here is an in depth listing of all the most common predators your birds may face and creative ways to counteract the treat that they pose to your wonderful little chickens.

Possums

These sneaky little critters only come out at night when no one is around. It's rare when you run into them, and it's even rarer when you catch them in the act of raiding your hen house. But they do steal chickens nonetheless. These animals are similar in size to the common housecat. They also have cat-like claws as well, which they use quite proficiently when it comes to slicing up chickens. To get rid of these try putting some ammonia drenched rags around the chicken coop. Possums can't stand the scent of ammonia and will ultimately be driven away by the odor.

Snakes

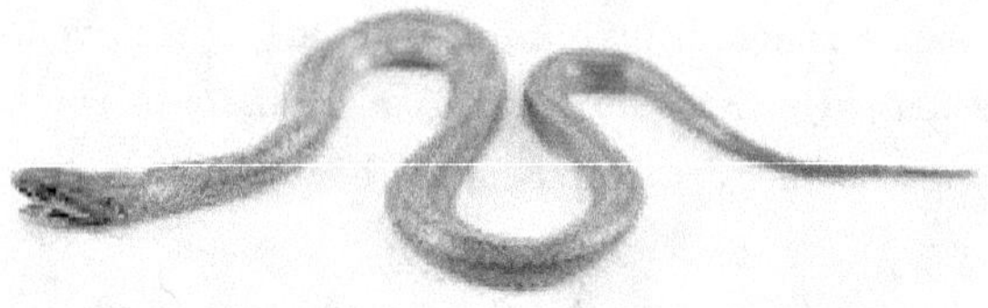

Snakes can be a real nuisance. They like to slither into coops and wolf down chicken eggs, but they can be fairly easily stopped in their slithering tracks. All you have to do is block their entrance to the coop. This means securing all potential entry points and putting up effective snake barriers such as thick hardware mesh that snakes are unable to cross. This will keep those serpents at bay.

Cats

Cats are everywhere and by sheer numbers alone, make up a fairly common threat. Cats pounce on chickens and use their claws to slit their throats. They often kill the birds just for fun, fulfilling their hunting instincts, and some even eat the chickens. The best way to get rid of cats is to use a high enough chicken wire fence to make sure they can't enter the hen house.

<u>Coyotes</u>

Depending on where you live, coyotes may be prowling around late at night looking to make a quick snack out of your chickens. They typically corner a bird and grab it by the neck, running away with the chicken hanging out of their mouth. To protect your birds from this threat, make sure that all of them stay in the coop at night. Also, raise your coop off the ground, and shield it with chicken wire. This should help to thwart coyote attacks.

<u>Raccoons</u>

Raccoons like to pay periodic visits to chicken coops for both eggs and chicken meat. These animals are very crafty, and often find secret ways to gain access to chicken coops. With these tricky animals all you can do is secure your coop as well as possible and hope for the best.

<u>*Foxes*</u>

The fox is a very smart animal, and will strategically watch and wait until they know they can single out a chicken for a meal. These animals are actually able to keep a clear mental record of exactly how many times a day you leave, and when it is you will most likely be gone. It is then that the strike. You can outfox the fox however. Strong hardware mesh may be enough to keep them at bay, and if not, you may want to move on to some good electric fencing.

Conclusion: From the Farm to Your Backyard

You don't have to have a major farming operation in order to enjoy the rewarding experience of raising chickens. As long as you have a modest sized backyard, you too can reap the benefits that chickens provide. I hope that this book has enlightened you with plenty of tips and tricks to get started. Now it's just up to you, to bring the best of the farm, right to your backyard. Thank you for reading!